HOW TO TURN YOUR TALENT INTO A BUSINESS

Easy steps for turning your talents into profit

TAUGHT BY
JANET GREEN

YES, you have what it takes to start your own business!
Let's birth it together and remember…
with GOD, ALL things are possible!

2011 © Olmstead Publishing

How to Turn Your Talent Into a Business
By Janet Green
howto@janetbusiness.com
www.janetbusiness.com
Front Cover Sketch by Therisiah Ngang   **GOD Did It!**

Cover and Formatting by Dr Phyllis M Olmstead

All rights reserved. No part of this book may be reproduced or transmitted in any form or by any means, electronic or mechanical, including photocopying, recording, or any information storage and retrieval system, without permission in writing from the publisher.

Olmstead Publishing
www.olmsteadpublishing.com
apopka@usa.com

Prayer

Father God I come to you with thanksgiving and praise. I thank You for all You have done in my life and all that You are about to do. I acknowledge You as my Savior, Provider, Healer, Protector, and my All In All.

As I step out in faith to do what You have called me to do, I ask for Your guidance, knowledge, wisdom, understanding, grace, protection, divine connections, and divine favor.

I thank You, in advance, as I glorify You, in Jesus' name, Amen.

Thank you, Jesus! Thank you, Lord!

Dedication

To my amazing children, Dejohn, Tevano, and Geovano Green, your labor of love towards this ministry has been amazing. Yes, as you always say, "When Mom starts a project that means we start it, too." As I delegated to you the different "behind the scene" responsibilities of this ministry, you never complained; instead, you carried out the different tasks with excellence. Thanks for helping to make this ministry a success and I love you all.

Objectives

- Learn the importance of "Putting God First" in everything you do
- Develop a more mature and spiritual "you"
- Listen to God's voice for direction
- Develop your physical being
- Disconnect from dream-killers and negative people
- Understand the concept of tithing both talents and finances
- Communicate your dreams of owning your own business with your significant other or immediate family members
- Select a mentor
- Have a vital prayer life
- Learn the fundamentals of starting your own business
- Develop a business plan
- Commit to "Business Networking"

- Determine the legal structure of your business
- Register your business
- Choose your business location
- Market your goods or services
- Select appropriate social media for business growth
- Connect with positive business-minded people
- Select and retain the most qualified workforce at an optimum performance level
- Learn the responsibilities of being an employer
- Prepare your start-up expense worksheet
- Stay faithful to your dream

Table of Contents

DEDICATION 4
OBJECTIVES 5
TABLE OF CONTENTS 7
AUTHOR 10
ACKNOWLEDGEMENTS 16
PREFACE 21
   I. FOUNDATION OF A SUCCESSFUL YOU 25

    MENTAL 29

    PHYSICAL 32

    TITHING 33

    SPIRITUAL 34

    FIVE KEYS TO FINANCIAL PROSPERITY AND A SUCCESSFUL BUSINESS 35

    CHAPTER ONE ASSIGNMENT 39

    DAILY DECLARATION 42

   II. PERSONAL DEVELOPMENT 48

    GRUDGE EXERCISE 51

    SELECT A PRAYER PARTNER 52

EFFECTIVE PRAYER 57
III. BUSINESS PLAN OUTLINE 61

WRITING YOUR BUSINESS PLAN 61

YOUR BUSINESS PLAN 62

Components of a Business Plan 64

Mock Business Plan 68

CHAPTER THREE ASSIGNMENT 84
IV. FORMING YOUR BUSINESS 85

DETERMINE THE LEGAL STRUCTURE OF YOUR BUSINESS 85

REGISTERING YOUR BUSINESS 87

CHAPTER FOUR ASSIGNMENT 89
V. HOW TO CHOOSE YOUR BUSINESS LOCATION 91

CHAPTER FIVE ASSIGNMENT 94
VI. POSITIONING YOUR BUSINESS FOR SUCCESS 96

ADVERTIZING AND MARKETING YOUR BUSINESS 96

SOCIAL MEDIA 101

CHAPTER SIX ASSIGNMENT 102
VII. SELECTING A SUCCESSFUL TEAM **104**

    MAKING THE RIGHT HIRING DECISIONS 104

    NOW YOU ARE READY TO PROCEED WITH INTERVIEWS 105

    MAINTAINING YOUR WORKFORCE 108

    EMPLOYER'S LEGAL RESPONSIBILITIES 112

    CHAPTER SEVEN ASSIGNMENT 114
VIII. YOUR BUSINESS STARTUP EXPENSE **116**

    CHAPTER EIGHT ASSIGNMENT 119
IX. GROWING YOUR BUSINESS **121**

    SUCCESSFUL NETWORKING 121

    GETTING PREPARED FOR A NETWORKING EVENT 122

    CHAPTER NINE ASSIGNMENT 125
X. STAY ENCOURAGED **127**

    BUILD YOUR NETWORKING GROUP 129
INDEX **139**
NOTES **140**

AUTHOR

Janet Green worked over twenty years in the hospitality industry. She started her career at a five star hotel in New York City as a PBX operator. After working six months, she was promoted to PBX supervisor, where she supervised 32 operators.

Even though she was the youngest staff member and had the fewest years of experience in her department, Janet did not let all the negative and spiteful words from her coworkers kill her enthusiasm. Instead, she used it as fuel to keep her fire burning. After only three months in that position, she was able to gain the respect and loyalty of her staff. Three years later, the company promoted her to front office supervisor.

As if this did not keep her busy enough, she took on some of the human resources department responsibilities, such as planning the annual associate picnic and holiday party for their four hundred-plus associates.

Janet's general manager saw great potential in her as a director of human resources (HR) and encouraged her to start a career in the field. She transferred to HR where she spent the next two years learning all the disciplines (recruiting, employee relations, employee benefits, and payroll) in that field. She then transferred to another state as an HR Manager and one year later, she became Director of Human Resources.

As busy as she was as a Director of Human Resources, Janet consistently exemplified the importance of giving back to the community. In one year, she was able to accomplish the following:

- Fed 1,767 homeless men and children
- Collected over 100 cellular phones for the "Secure A Call Foundation"
- Collected over 65 pairs of used eye glasses for donations
- Collected over 112 pairs of used sneakers to refurbish tennis courts
- Raised funds for the "Children's Miracle Network"
- Planned and executed a hotel market picnic for over 3,000 associates and families

In July of 2009, Janet experienced the worst year of her professional career. At that time, she began to strengthen her relationship with God through prayer.

One day she prayed and asked God to close all doors that needed to be closed and to open all the doors that needed to be opened in her life. Fewer than 48 hours later, Janet noticed what she described as "all hell breaking loose" around her. First, her career as Director of Human Resources ended abruptly and 24 hours after that, her fiancé called to end their three-year relationship.

Janet then turned to God for answers as to why it seemed that everything was going wrong in her life, and then she remembered how good God is and immediately began to thank Him for her life and the lives of her sons. On the third night of this turn-of-events, God told Janet in a dream, "'You prayed for me to close all doors that needed to be closed and to open all doors that needed to be opened' and I answered your prayer." From that day forth, Janet was at peace with the things happening in her life.

Janet then decided it was time for her to start her own business. Even though it was no secret in her family that she was a gifted cook and had the wits of a tough business woman, they were disappointed that she would no longer do what she did best, taking care of others and defending the voiceless as a director of human resources.

In July of 2009, Janet started Jamaican Global Throw Down Catering Services. She started with the concept of catering for weddings, parties, and reunions. As she researched the food industry and catering business market, she realized that there were endless possibilities for her services and products. During her first year in business, she volunteered her time cooking at least monthly for charitable organizations. Her motto is "Anyone that eats is my customer." Janet also became a member of several chambers of commerce in the local Orlando, Florida area.

Approximately eight months later Janet got a vision from God to head the Entrepreneur Ministry at New Destiny Christian Center. She tried to negotiate with God by telling Him she could do a better job helping the ministry and not leading it, but when God reminded her of the story of Jonah, she surrendered. Janet then fasted and prayed for God's direction as she started to put together the materials she would teach, eventually becoming this book. Janet held the first Entrepreneur Class at New Destiny, "How to Start Your Business" in April of 2010 with 40 students. As if she was not busy enough, the single mom continues to mentor her three sons: De'John, Tevano, and Geovano Green. She often says her first love is God and her second love is her three boys.

Acknowledgements

I want to thank my pastor, Dr. Zachery Tims, of the New Destiny Christian Center in Apopka, Florida, who has allowed me to direct the Entrepreneur Ministry, the exact place where I started this new chapter in my life. Thank you, sir, for your support!

To Elder Marguerite Esannason, thanks for all you do. To Minister Richard Harvey, who is always there to support the Ministry at our New Business Birthing and Networking celebrations, I thank you, sir. To Minister Samuel Anderson, who listened to my ideas and consistently spoke words of support over this ministry, I thank you, sir. Minister Anderson, not only do you speak positive works of support to this ministry but you are always at our events speaking with the new business owners and encouraging them, and for that, I salute you, sir.

Dr. Robert Spooney, President of the African American Chamber of Commerce, Orlando, I am so grateful to you for teaching the students how to sell their businesses and the positive words you have planted in their lives. Pamela Martin, Office Manager African American Chamber, I appreciate all your support and prayers. Mr. Howard Walker, I appreciate your wealth of knowledge on 501(c) businesses. Mr. Errick Young, Manager for Orange County Business Development, I greatly appreciate the time you spent connecting these new business owners to seasoned business owners, and mentoring and guiding them as they entered the world of business. "Lady D," the host of WOBK Radio 1680AM and TV Talk Show Host, I love you and appreciate all the air time you have given to this ministry, and the time you have spent emceeing our networking events. Mr. Glenn Allgood, Allgood Entertainment, and Ms. Shanti

Persaud-Hernandez, General Manager of WOKB 1680AM Radio, much gratitude to you in promoting this ministry's events.

I am so grateful to all business owners who have taken this class and have successfully started your own businesses. I thank you for confirming the need for this class in our community. Your testimonies of God's divine favor and divine connections validate that God is leading this ministry to great success. To Elizabeth Pinkston, Janet Coke, Marvo Irons, Patricia Betancourt, Sonia Troupe, Mr. and Mrs. Chris Assanah, and Mr. and Mrs. Roosevelt Adams, thank you for your encouraging words, your prayers, and your labor of love towards this ministry.

To Bishop TD Jakes, Dr. Darlean Thomas, and Joyce Meyers, I am so grateful for your ministries, which helped me to birth this book. To John Locanto, Regional VP of Hotel Groups, and Don Fraser, GM, I thank you for the six best years of my career as Director of Human Resources.

To Hope Bethune, one of my Prayer Warriors, I love you and thank you for all your prayers. To all the New Destiny Christian Center volunteers who have worked our networking events, thank you for your labor of love. I greatly appreciate you.

To my incredible parents, Valrey and Wesley Smith, thanks for always having my back, loving me unconditionally, and seeing the good in me. I love you both! I could not have asked God for better parents.

Finally to Kes and Nadine Smith (my brother Kes is one of my prayer warriors, a wonderful man of God), thanks for listening to me, praying with me and guiding me biblically throughout this journey. I love both you and your wife and may God continue to richly bless your marriage.

Preface

To all my readers, I wrote this book for everyone who wants to start his or her own business. There is no age limit, culture limit, no gender restriction, educational demands, and most importantly, denominational requirements. In other words, if you are want to start your own business this book was written for you. I prayed and fasted prior to writing this book. I have asked God to speak to the hearts of His people and let them know that it is through divine favor and divine appointment that they have purchased this book, or was blessed with this book. I prayed to God that He would give each of you visions of confirmation that this is your season to start your business. God, let me know that you are going through a season in your life that is signaling it is time for you to make changes in your life. This is the season that God has created for us. Let us embrace it positively. Let us seek His guidance and a closer relationship with Him as He guides us to another level. Let us come together and unite as God's children doing Kingdom business. Let us help each other. Let us support each other and finally, let us love each other the way God intended.

Remember that God has already equipped us with the tools we need to make the first move:

📖 Deuteronomy 8:18, (KJV) [18]But thou shalt remember the LORD thy God: for it is he that giveth thee power to get wealth that he may establish his covenant which he sware unto thy fathers, as it is this day.

📖 Psalm 37:4, (KJV), [4]Delight thyself also in the LORD: and he shall give thee the desires of thine heart.

📖 Isaiah 1:19, (KJV) ¹⁹If ye be willing and obedient, ye shall eat the good of the land.

🕯 Pray and ask God to let you know what His will for your life is. Remember, God's will for our lives is always best. Submit yourself to God and ask for His grace and guidance as you start your new journey. It is imperative that you maintain a relationship with God, surround yourself with positive people, sow financial seeds, and sow your talents. Be focused and believe in your dream. In addition, most of all have faith and believe God.

If you apply all of the principles in this book, you will be successful in whatever business you start. Do not focus on where you are but look towards your goal. You cannot run a race looking backwards. You have to position yourself by looking forward and moving forward.

Every one of us has at least one gift and talent from God. 📖 Ephesians 4:6-8 (KJV) ⁶One God and Father of all, who is above all, and through all, and in you all. ⁷But unto every one of us is given grace according to the measure of the gift of Christ. ⁸Wherefore he saith, When he ascended up on high, he led captivity captive, and gave gifts unto men.

Be sure to leverage what you have for what you need.

May God bless you and guide you as you pursue your business.

Chapter One

Foundation of a Successful You

To help you determine what business to start ask yourself the following questions:

1. What do I do well?
2. What do I enjoy doing?
3. What do I enjoy doing that I would do for free?
4. What do I perform effortlessly while others struggle to do it?

Now that you know what your talent is let us see how we can turn it into a business. You should be clear on **why** you want to start this business and with **who**m you want to do business. In other words, **who** will be your target customers? Money should not be your number one reason for starting a business because this could diminish your focus on excellence. You should have a passion for what you do because your passion will translate into dollars.

The first two chapters of this book deal with preparing you mentally, physically, and spiritually. This book will also instruct you on how to become a successful business owner, so relax and enjoy the journey.

Chapters One and Two deal with laying the foundation. Once the foundation is solid, nothing can destroy its structure. For all the long hours that you will invest in your business, if you include exercise in your day-to-day routine you will be better able to cope with the stress **(Physical)**.

As you develop a greater relationship with God, you can hear Him more clearly as He directs you on a daily basis. You will also learn how to better prepare yourself for divine favor and not miss your visitations **(Spiritual)**.

As you release all the hatred in your system, you will make way for God to release all the blessings He has in store for you. It is like a clogged up sink, the water will flow extremely slow, but as soon as you clear the clog, it flows freely **(Mental)**. More importantly, you will need to start sowing seeds.

Choose a ministry in your church where you can sow your talent. If the ministry that you are interested in does not exist, start one. If starting a ministry now is not practical then volunteer at a hospital, nursing home, or a youth center. You also need to give 10% of all your wages or earnings to the church where you worship. If you do not have a home church and you consistently watch a church service on the Internet or on TV then you should give 10% of your income to that ministry. Giving an offering is highly recommended, also. Remember, you cannot out give God 💰 **(Tithe)**.

The four areas of our lives that we need to focus on are as follows:

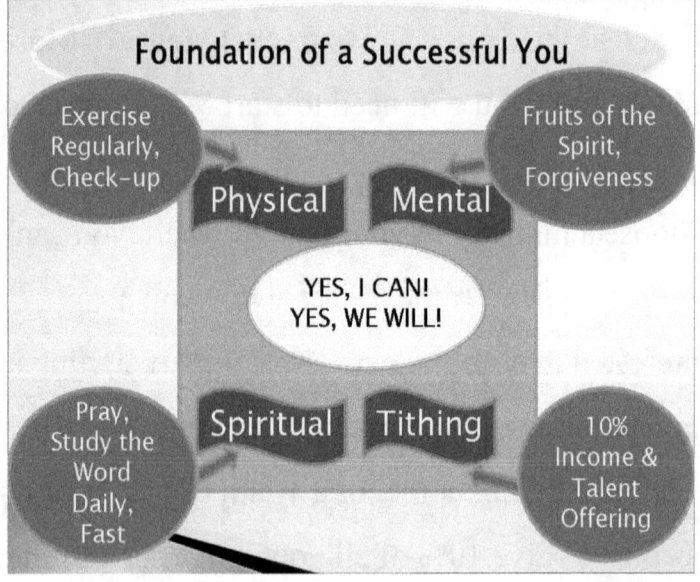

Mental

I believe a positive state of mind produces a sense of well being that allows a person to function effectively in the world system, in my humble opinion. People who are mentally healthy are well adjusted to society, are able to relate well to others, and feel satisfied with themselves and their role in the world. In researching for this book, I compiled a definition of mental health from various sources. The definition I developed reads: a state of well-being in which the individual realizes his or her own abilities, can cope with the normal stresses of life, can work productively and fruitfully, and is able to contribute to his or her community. From a biblical standpoint, I have provided several Bible verses below that will help you understand God's truth concerning mental health. I think of this as cleaning out the blockages in our lives that prevent the blessings of God from freely flowing. Think of it as a clogged sink, if you do not clean it out, it will eventually stop flowing.

📖 Galatians 5:22-26 (KJV) [22]But the fruit of the Spirit is love, joy, peace, longsuffering, gentleness, goodness, faith, [23]Meekness, temperance: against such there is no law. [24]And they that are Christ's have crucified the flesh with the affections and lusts. [25]If we live in the Spirit, let us also walk in the Spirit. [26]Let us not be desirous of vain glory, provoking one another, envying one another.

📖 Matthew 5:44 (KJV) [44]But I say unto you, Love your enemies, bless them that curse you, do good to them that hate you, and pray for them which despitefully use you, and persecute you;

📖 Matthew 6:14 (KJV) ¹⁴For if ye forgive men their trespasses, your heavenly Father will also forgive you:

📖 James 2:14 (KJV) ¹⁴What doth it profit, my brethren, though a man say he hath faith, and have not works? can faith save him?

📖 Romans 12:14-19 (KJV) ¹⁴Bless them which persecute you: bless, and curse not. ¹⁵Rejoice with them that do rejoice, and weep with them that weep. ¹⁶Be of the same mind one toward another. Mind not high things, but condescend to men of low estate. Be not wise in your own conceits. ¹⁷Recompense to no man evil for evil. Provide things honest in the sight of all men. ¹⁸If it be possible, as much as lieth in you, live peaceably with all men. ¹⁹Dearly beloved, avenge not yourselves, but rather give place unto wrath: for it is written, Vengeance is mine; I will repay, saith the Lord.

Physical

As you start planning your business, you will find yourself working long hours. Remember to schedule at least thirty minutes per day to exercise. This helps to clear your mind.

📖 1 Corinthians 6:19 (KJV) [19]What? know ye not that your body is the temple of the Holy Ghost which is in you, which ye have of God, and ye are not your own?

📖 2 Corinthians 6:16 (KJV) [16]And what agreement hath the temple of God with idols? for ye are the temple of the living God; as God hath said, I will dwell in them, and walk in them; and I will be their God, and they shall be my people.

📖 1 Corinthians 3:16 (KJV) ¹⁶Know ye not that ye are the temple of God, and that the Spirit of God dwelleth in you?

Tithing

You have to sow a seed to reap a harvest. You cannot walk into a store and receive goods or services and leave without paying for them. You have to give something to get something.

📖 Malachi 3:8 (KJV) ⁸Will a man rob God? Yet ye have robbed me. But ye say, Wherein have we robbed thee? In tithes and offerings.

📖 Proverbs 3:9 (KJV) ⁹Honour the LORD with thy substance, and with the firstfruits of all thine increase:

📖 Leviticus 27:30 (KJV) ³⁰And all the tithe of the land, whether of the seed of the land, or of the fruit of the tree, is the LORD's: it is holy unto the LORD.

📖 Matthew 5:23-24 (KJV) [23]Therefore if thou bring thy gift to the altar, and there rememberest that thy brother hath ought against thee; [24]Leave there thy gift before the altar, and go thy way; first be reconciled to thy brother, and then come and offer thy gift.

Spiritual

Your relationship with God can help you gain insight on how to approach situations. It will also give you a sense of peace, victory, strength in your faith, divine favor, visitations, mental clarity, anointing, knowledge, wisdom, and understanding. How can we develop these areas? All of these can be accomplished through spending more time with God; fasting, praying, and reading the Bible.

📖 2 Corinthians 11:27 (KJV) ²⁷In weariness and painfulness, in watchings often, in hunger and thirst, in fastings often, in cold and nakedness.

📖 Matthew 17:21 (KJV) ²¹Howbeit this kind goeth not out but by prayer and fasting.

📖 Isaiah 40:29 (KJV) ²⁹He giveth power to the faint; and to them that have no might he increaseth strength.

📖 Psalm 37:5 (KJV) ⁵Commit thy way unto the LORD; trust also in him; and he shall bring it to pass.

Five keys to Financial Prosperity and a Successful Business

1. Put **God First** in everything you do.
2. Be willing to be used by God and be obedient to His Word, even when it does

not make sense to you. We must always be submissive to God, who is our Creator.

3. Have a positive mind-set. Know that God is always in control. Everything works together for our good.
4. You **must** sow seeds to reap a harvest.
5. As God blesses you be a blessing to someone else.

📖 Genesis 8:22 (KJV) ²²While the earth remaineth, seedtime and harvest, and cold and heat, and summer and winter, and day and night shall not cease.

📖 Luke 5:1-7 (KJV) ¹And it came to pass, that, as the people pressed upon him to hear the word of God, he stood by the lake of Gennesaret, ²And saw two ships standing by the lake: but the fishermen were gone out of them, and were washing their nets. ³And he entered into one of the ships, which was Simon's, and prayed him that he would thrust out a little from the land. And he sat down, and taught the people out of the ship. *(Be willing to be used by God and be obedient to God's word. Be submissive to God).*

⁴Now when he had left speaking, he said unto Simon, Launch out into the deep, and let down your nets for a draught. ⁵And Simon answering said unto him, Master, we have toiled all the night, and have taken nothing: nevertheless at thy word I will let down the net. *(Trust God and have a positive mindset. Know that God is always in control and everything works together for our good. It does not have to make sense to you.)*

⁶And when they had this done, they inclosed a great multitude of fishes: and their net brake. ⁷And they beckoned unto their partners, which were in

the other ship, that they should come and help them. And they came, and filled both the ships, so that they began to sink. *(Bless someone else whenever God blesses you.)*

God is always talking to us. Are we listening to Him? What is our response? *Allow yourself to be used by God and be obedient to His words.*

Chapter One Assignment

- Exercise at least 15 minutes per day for six days per week. Start with a light exercise such as walking. Please consult your Physician before starting any exercise program.
- Spend quality time with God each day by praying and reading His Word (increase this time daily).
- Start to disconnect from all your negative associations.
- Start to develop positive associations.
- Fast at least one day this week.

  - Asking God to close all doors that need to be closed and to open doors that need to be opened in your life, according to His will. Warning …You must be ready for changes before you pray this prayer (See prayer below).

- Ask God for His guidance and direction for your new business according to His will.
- Pray and ask God to develop your hearing so you can hear His voice clearly.
- Pray and ask God for the knowledge, wisdom, grace, and understanding to start this new venture.

🕊 Start sowing seeds with your talent. Sign up to volunteer in a ministry at your church, local hospital or school.

📖 Read Psalm 1 and Psalm 91 daily.

📖 Prayer

Father God I come to you with thanksgiving and praises. I thank You for all You have done in my life and all that You are about to do. I acknowledge You as my Savior, Provider, Healer, Protector, and my All In All. Heavenly Father, I come to You in Jesus Christ's Holy Name. I ask You Lord Jesus Christ according to 📖 John 14:13-14, (KJV) '[13]And whatsoever ye shall ask in my name, that will I do, that the Father may be glorified in the Son. [14]If ye shall ask any thing in my name, I will do it.' I ask that You close all doors that need to be closed in my life and open all doors that need to be opened in my life according to your will for my life, in Jesus' name I pray. Amen.

Thank you Jesus! Thank you Lord!

Daily Declaration

Read the following declarations daily, as they will help to strengthen your relationship with God.

📖 Matthew 7:7-8, (KJV) [7]Ask, and it shall be given you; seek, and ye shall find; knock, and it shall be opened unto you: [8]For every one that asketh receiveth; and he that seeketh findeth; and to him that knocketh it shall be opened.

📖 Proverbs 11:27, (KJV) [27]He that diligently seeketh good procureth favour: but he that seeketh mischief, it shall come unto him.

📖 Matthew 17:20, (KJV) [20]And Jesus said unto them, Because of your unbelief: for verily I say unto you, If ye have faith as a grain of mustard seed, ye shall say unto this mountain, Remove hence to yonder place; and it shall remove; and nothing shall be impossible unto you.

📖 Luke 6:38, (KJV) [38]Give, and it shall be given unto you; good measure, pressed down, and shaken together, and running over, shall men give into your bosom. For with the same measure that ye mete withal it shall be measured to you again.

📖 Luke 1:28, (KJV) [28]And the angel came in unto her, and said, Hail, thou that art highly favoured, the Lord is with thee: blessed art thou among women.

📖 Deuteronomy 8:18, (KJV) [18]But thou shalt remember the LORD thy God: for it is he that giveth thee power to get wealth, that he may establish his covenant which he sware unto thy fathers, as it is this day.

📖 Psalm 112:3, (KJV) ³Wealth and riches shall be in his house: and his righteousness endureth for ever.

📖 2 Corinthians 9:8, (KJV) ⁸And God is able to make all grace abound toward you; that ye, always having all sufficiency in all things, may abound to every good work:

📖 1 Peter 5:7, (KJV) ⁷Casting all your care upon him; for he careth for you.

📖 Psalm 1:3, (KJV) ³And he shall be like a tree planted by the rivers of water, that bringeth forth his fruit in his season; his leaf also shall not wither; and whatsoever he doeth shall prosper.

📖 Proverbs 10:22, (KJV) ²²The blessing of the LORD, it maketh rich, and he addeth no sorrow with it.

📖 Deuteronomy 28:8, (KJV) ⁸The LORD shall command the blessing upon thee in thy storehouses, and in all that thou settest thine hand unto; and he shall bless thee in the land which the LORD thy God giveth thee.

📖 Psalm 37:4, (KJV) ⁴Delight thyself also in the LORD: and he shall give thee the desires of thine heart.

📖 Malachi 3:10-11, (KJV) ¹⁰Bring ye all the tithes into the storehouse, that there may be meat in mine house, and prove me now herewith, saith the LORD of hosts, if I will not open you the windows of heaven, and pour you out a blessing, that there shall not be room enough to receive it. ¹¹And I will rebuke the devourer for your sakes, and he shall not destroy the fruits of your ground; neither shall your vine cast her fruit before the time in the field, saith the LORD of hosts.

📖 Isaiah 54:17, (KJV) [17]No weapon that is formed against thee shall prosper; and every tongue that shall rise against thee in judgment thou shalt condemn. This is the heritage of the servants of the LORD, and their righteousness is of me, saith the LORD.

📖 3 John 1:2, (KJV) [2]Beloved, I wish above all things that thou mayest prosper and be in health, even as thy soul prospereth.

📖 Deuteronomy 28:1, (KJV) [1]And it shall come to pass, if thou shalt hearken diligently unto the voice of the LORD thy God, to observe and to do all his commandments which I command thee this day, that the LORD thy God will set thee on high above all nations of the earth

📖 Deuteronomy 28:12, (KJV) [12]The LORD shall open unto thee his good treasure, the heaven to give the rain unto thy land in his season, and to bless all the work of thine hand: and thou shalt lend unto many nations, and thou shalt not borrow.

Chapter Two

Personal Development

For the next seven days, honestly complete the following exercise. Do not adjust your habits so that this exercise will look good on paper. You are the only person who will see it. Once you have completed the exercise, take a few minutes carefully examining how you spend your time. Please be reminded that your rest is as important as your work habit.

My Time Spent Per 24 Hours

	TV/ Internet	Family/ Work	Self/ Exercise	Prayer Meditation, Word	Sleep
Mon					
Tue					
Wed					
Thu					
Fri					
Sat					
Sun					

List the first names of people you speak with more than twice per week. Indicate which Discussion Topics you conversed with each person regarding.

First Name	Discussion Topics		
	Business	Spirituality	Other, People

Grudge Exercise.

Schedule forty minutes of uninterrupted time to complete this exercise. Take five minutes to think about everyone with which you have a grudge. Write their names on a piece of paper. Give yourself permission to forgive them. As you rip the paper into small pieces, pray and thank God for giving you the courage to forgive each person. Ask God to give you the strength, courage, and grace as you reach out to each person for forgiveness. Speak to the individuals and ask them for forgiveness. Release them or the situation and then pray and thank God that you are able to forgive and move towards His plan for your life. Wow! What a liberating feeling. Do not rob yourself of God's ultimate blessings for your life. **Complete the prior exercise before proceeding to the next chapter.**

Select a Prayer Partner

A prayer partner should believe in the dreams and visions you have for your business. He or she should be spiritually connected to God. You both should pray together at least once a week (choose someone of the same gender). Take a week to pray for someone else. During this week, fast from praying for yourself because your prayer partner should be praying for you. Remember the story of Job? God turned his situation around when he prayed for someone else.

📖 Read Psalm 23 (KJV) with your prayer partner and personalize it for each other (insert your prayer partner's name wherever the name Janet appears).

[1]The LORD is **my** (Janet) shepherd; *I* (Janet) shall not want.
[2]He maketh **me** (Janet) to lie down in green

pastures: he leadeth **me** (Janet) beside the still waters.

³He restoreth **my** (Janet) soul: he leadeth **me** (Janet) in the paths of righteousness for his name's sake.

⁴Yea, though **I** (Janet) walk through the valley of the shadow of death, **I** (Janet) will fear no evil: for thou art with **me** (Janet); thy rod and thy staff they comfort **me** (Janet).

⁵Thou preparest a table before **me** (Janet) in the presence of **mine** (Janet) enemies: thou anointest **my** (Janet) head with oil; **my** (Janet) cup runneth over.

⁶Surely goodness and mercy shall follow **me** (Janet) all the days of **my** (Janet) life: and **I** (Janet) will dwell in the house of the LORD for ever.

Ask yourself the following questions. If your responses are 'Yes,' then you are on the right track.

- Can I use my gifts and talents in this business?
- Do I enjoy performing the duties in this business?
- Has God communicated with me regarding this venture?
- Would I perform the activities in this business for free?
- Do I have a passion for this business?

Meet with your immediate family members or highly trusted friends to communicate your business venture and solicit their help.

Be mindful that this vision is from God to you. Your family members will not have the same level of excitement that you have or the level of understanding for this business venture. Do not be disappointed if they do not embrace your new venture with the same level of excitement you have. Instead, stay positive and express how important it would be to you for them to support your new venture. Allow them to ask questions and answer their questions honestly. Give all family members an assignment according to their gifts, abilities, and personalities. This will allow them to feel as if they are a part of your new venture.

Family members and trusted friends can help you with your new business as follows:

- Suggest names for your new business
- Suggest logos for your new business
- Suggest mission statements for your new business

- For younger kids have them research similar businesses on the Internet and report their findings on company policies and procedures.
- Schedule a time to meet with family members to discuss progress.
- Pray before and after each meeting.
- Do not schedule meetings during times when other family member have previous engagements (they may develop a resentment towards your mission).
- Meeting days and times should be agreed upon by all members.
- Allow each family member to report their assignment results.
- Be positive, and honest about each member's feedback.

Effective Prayer

- Always start your prayers with thanksgiving. Make your requests known to God (reminder God's will for your life is always better) and end your prayer with, "In Jesus name I pray amen"
- Ask God to give you the grace to not miss your visitations
- Plant a seed
- Command the devil to loose his hands off your finances, health, and children or whatever you believe God for.
- Claim it
- Dispatch ministering angels to gather your harvest
- Speak yourself into the future or what you believe God for and do not live by your circumstances.

- Begin to believe that God has answered your prayers by praising and thanking Him in advance.

Be patient and wait for God to fulfill your requests according to His will. Be sure to praise God as you wait. Reminder: God's timeframe is not our timeframe.

Chapter Two Assignment

- ✝ Exercise at least 20 minutes a day for five days per week.
- ✝ Spend quality time with God each day thanking him for this new venture.
- ✝ Begin to praise God and thank Him for answering your prayers.
- ✝ Thank God for choosing you for this business venture.
- ✝ Loose all your negative associations.
- ✝ Continue to develop positive associations.
- ✝ Meet with your immediate family members to communicate your new business venture and solicit their help (pray before and after your meeting). Schedule a meeting time and place that is suitable for everyone involved.
- ✝ Fast at least one day this week.

🕊 Continue sowing seeds with your talents and offerings.

💰 Give your tithe (10% of all income you receive).

📖 Read Psalm 1 and Psalm 91 daily.

Chapter Three

Business Plan Outline

Writing Your Business Plan

Speak with people, both successful and not so successful within your line of business. Filter the information you received (use the information that will help your business and disregard any information that is not necessary for the success of your business). Record the best practices of other businesses and note their reasons for failure. This information will be crucial because as you build your business you could implement your great ideas and not repeat the poor decisions that cause businesses to fail.

Select a Business Mentor, this should be someone that supports your dream and believes in your success. Do not be in a rush to select a mentor, wait on God's divine direction and He will make the divine connection.

Your Business Plan

Your Business Plan is the blueprint for your business. Therefore, you should spend quality time working on clearly defining your business model. Use clear and simple language to communicate your ideas, and visions. A well-written business plan will play a key role in the success of your business. You will also need your business plan for loans and certifications.

Make sure you have a passion for owning the business you plan to start. You should always pray before you start your Business Plan and schedule uninterrupted time to formulate your ideas. Do not be frustrated if an idea does not flow, just trust

God, because He is in control. Your ideas for your business will flow when the time is right. Be sure to work on your business plan at the time of day when you function best. If you function best as a "morning person," then schedule uninterrupted time in the morning to work on your Business Plan.

Be willing to solicit ideas from other successful small and large businesses, family members, government agencies, and your mentor. Visit your local SCORE chapter and Small Business Administration (SBA 1800-U-ASK-SBA; WWW.SBA.GOV) office. Learn everything you can about the business you want to establish. Research your business ideas to determine if there is a need for your services or products. Utilize the following sources for gathering statistical and demographical information:

- Internet
- Chamber of Commerce
- Libraries and published directories
- Family and friends
- Small Business Administration

Study and evaluate your competitors and keep accurate records of your findings. Test your ideas with potential customers, friends, and family members who can offer constructive feedback. Be prepared to make changes to your Business Plan based on feedback you received after you have validate the information.

Components of a Business Plan

Company Description

- Mission Statement
- Company Goals and Objectives

- Business Philosophy
- Future Plans

Industry Analysis

- Catering/Restaurant Industry
- Future Trends and Strategic Opportunities
- Company Strengths and Core Competencies

Related Services and Products

- The Menu
- Production
- Services

Target Market Sector

- Three Major Segments

- Customer Profiles
- Competitive Strategy

Marketing Plan and Strategy

- Market Penetration
- Marketing Strategy
- Marketing Plan
- Effort

Operations

- Employee Training and Education
- System and Controls
- Food Production
- Delivery Service

Management and Organization

- Management Structure
- Ownership
- Milestone
- Risk Evaluation

Appendices

- Menu

Mock Business Plan

Company Description

JGTDXX is a unique family owned and operated Caribbean Restaurant with a highly motivated staff and stellar customer service. We provide the most appetizing Caribbean food in central Florida. Our staff has over 20 years of combined customer service experience in the hospitality and food industry. JGTDXX specializes in blending other cultures with daily delights from around the world and our food specials are the highlight of our theme. We are also current members of several Chambers of Commerce in the central Florida area and Certified as a Minority Women Own Business Enterprise for Orange County.

Mission Statement

- Our company's goal is to focus on the success of the business, the high quality of food,

attitude, fairness, understanding, and generosity between management, staff, customers, and vendors
- We will promote and develop unity among cultures through food, while generating enthusiasm and excitement among each other.
- We will present a variety of dishes to the community that everyone will enjoy and find appetizing. Awareness of all these factors and the responsible actions that result will give our business a sense of purpose and meaning beyond our basic financial goals.

<u>Company's Goals and Objectives</u>
- All JGTDXX employees will take pride in providing our customers with world-class customer service while blessing their appetites with mouth-watering food.
- All team members will model the credo *"**Put God first in everything we do,**"* and this

means we will conduct business with integrity and treat our customers with the utmost respect.
- JGTDXX will become the most talked about restaurant because of our Christ-like manner, food, and our commitment to high-quality service and community involvement. We will tangibly commit to contribute to the community at large.

Business Philosophy
- Put God first in everything we do and have a passion for what we do
- Have a passion for people and to serve people
- To treat others as we would like to be treated

Target Market Sector
JGTDXX will market to families of all cultures and ethnicities in the surrounding communities. We will also be expanding to other areas,

communities, and states. The core principle our business is to *unite people through food.* We will offer a variety of foods, i.e., Jamaican, Chinese, Italian, and American.

Future Plans

When our business meets its overhead projections by our second year, we will start scouting for a second location in the Central Florida area and develop plans for the next restaurant unit. Our six-year goal is to have three restaurants in the Central Florida Region and to serve at least four different culturally diverse cuisines.

Industry Analysis

Although the restaurant industry is very competitive, the lifestyle changes created by modern living continue to fuel its steady growth. More and more people have less time, resources, and ability to cook for themselves. Trends are very important and JGTDXX is well positioned for the current market for quick meals at moderate to low prices.

The Restaurant Industry Today

I believe the food service business is the third largest industry in the country. It accounts for over $240 billion annually in sales and the independent restaurant sector accounts for 15% of that total. The average American spends 15% of his/her income on meals away from home. This number is steadily increasing. There are 600 new restaurants opening every month and over 200 more needed to keep pace with the increasing demand.

At our restaurant, patrons will be able to satisfy their appetites with whatever flavor they so desire, whether it be Jamaican, Chinese, Italian, or American cuisine.

Future Trends and Strategic Opportunities

I believe the predicted growth trend is very positive both in short and long-term projections. People will be compelled to eat more meals away from home because generation today is working two or more jobs and time does not permit them to cook.

Important Company Strengths and Core Competencies:

- Strengths
  - Cooking ability
  - Interpersonal skills
  - 20 years of hospitality experience
  - 15 years of food service experience
  - Customer service experience
  - Positive relationship with different chambers of commerce
- Core Competencies

- Food Service
- Hospitality
- Customer Service
- Accounting

Related Services and Products

JGTDXX Restaurant will offer a menu of food and beverages with a distinctive image. There will be four ways to purchase our products: table service at the restaurant, take-out from the restaurant, home or office delivery, and at catering events.

Menu

JGTDXX's menu is moderate in size and moderately priced. We offer a collection of Jamaican, Chinese, Italian, and American cuisine that is flavorful, and familiar. Our goal is to create the image of satisfying and nutritious food.

Production

Food production and assembly will take place in

restaurant's kitchen. Fresh vegetables, meat, and dairy products are some of the ingredients that will be used to create most of the dishes from scratch. The chef will implement strict standards of sanitation, quality food production and presentation, and/or packaging.

Service

There will be three ways a customer can purchase food. Customers may dine in and be serviced by a server. Customers may also pick up their food at our take-out counter. Most take-out food will be cooked to order with orders coming from via telephone or fax. Delivery service (an indirect form of take-out) will also be available at certain times and to limited areas.

Target Market Sector

The market for JGTDXX's products covers a large area of diverse and heavily populated groups. Our products will be marketed in areas that are surrounded by a lot of human traffic and by other businesses that will direct customers to our restaurant. This is an area where people travel by foot or car to eat out and one that is also frequented by tourists. It is also an area known for and caters to the demographic group we are targeting.

The customer base will come from three major segments:

- Local residents
- Tourists
- Local businesses

The food concept and product image of JGTDXX will attract several different customer profiles:

- Students and Singles
- Single Parents
- Multicultural Families
- The Health Conscious
- Food Lovers

Competitive Strategy and Business Philosophy

There are major ways in which we will create an advantage over our competitors:

- Put God first in everything we do and have a passion for what we do.
- Have a passion for people and to serve people
- Treat others as we would like to be treated
- Product identity, branding, quality, and uniqueness
- High employee motivation and good sales attitude (everyone is a sales person)
- Innovative and aggressive service options

Market Penetration

Entry into the market should not be a problem. We will utilize preopening advertising and public relations campaigns. In addition, as CEO, I will be visiting local Chambers of Commerce, churches, schools, small business organizations, networking events, and sending out email blasts.

Marketing Strategy

Because our central focus will be based on the unique aspect of the product theme, "tasty foods," a mix of marketing vehicles will be created to convey our presence, our image, and our message.

Marketing Plan:

Marketing research

Economics

Products

Features and Benefits

Customers

Competition

Niches

Strategies

Sales Forecast

Consistency is Key in Marketing

Print media - Newspapers, magazines, and student publications

Broadcast media - local programming and special interest shows, local radio

Networking – Charity and chamber of commerce events

Direct mail -- Subscriber lists, offices flyers (repeat every two weeks)

Social Media – Facebook®, Twitter®, LinkedIn®

Marketing Effort in Three Phases:

1) Opening: Flyers to businesses and residences; word-of-mouth.

2) Ongoing: Specials: sales, etc.

3) Point of sale -- A well-trained staff can increase the average check as well as enhance the customer's overall experience. Employee and customer referrals are very important factors in building a strong customer base.

Operations

Employee Training and Education on our products, services, and core values

Employees will be trained not only in their specific operational duties but also in the philosophy and applications of the overall company concept. Employees will know the menu ingredients, and will taste test all new items on the menu. We consider all employees "sales people."

Systems and Controls

A big emphasis is being placed on extensive research into the quality and integrity of our products. We will constantly test our products to maintain our own high standards of freshness and purity. We will use a computer system to track food costs and inventory control and then management will review accuracy.

Food Production

Our food will be prepared on company premises. The kitchen will meet our high standards of efficiency and sanitized daily. Our food will be made to order.

Delivery and Catering

Food for delivery may be similar to take-out (prepared to order) or it may be prepared earlier and stocked. If no servers are required, all catering orders will be treated as deliveries.

Management Structure

Janet G ….. President and Chief Operating Officer

Dee G…….. Assistant Chef

Tev G …….. Marketing Director

Geo G ……..Sales Person

Jullie S…… Accountant

Ownership

Janet G will retain 100 percent ownership.

Longterm Development

JGTDXX is an innovative concept that targets a new, growing market. We assume that the market will respond, and grow quickly in the next five years. Our goals are to create a reputation of quality, consistency, and security (food safety) that will make us the leader of a new style of dining.

Strategies

Our marketing efforts will be concentrated on take-out and delivery, the areas of most promising growth. As the market changes, new products may be added to maintain sales and keep up with the growing trends.

Milestones

After the restaurant opens, we will keep a close eye on all sales and profits. Three years later, we will look at expanding the restaurant.

Risk Evaluation

As with any new venture, there is risk involved. The success of our project hinges on the strength and acceptance of a new market. After the first year, we expect some copycat competition in the form of other independent units.

Chapter Three Assignment

- Exercise at least 25 minutes per day for five days a week.
- Spend quality time with God each day thanking Him for His direction with your new business.
- Start to formulate your business Goals and Objectives for your Business Plan.
- Thank God for closing all doors that need to be closed and for opening all doors that need to be opened in your life.
- Embrace your new positive associations.
- Thank God in advance for developing your hearing so you can hear Him speaking to you clearly.
- Continue sowing seeds with your talents and offerings.
- Give your tithe (10% of all income you receive).
- Read Psalm 1 and Psalm 91 daily.

Chapter Four

Forming Your Business

Determine the Legal Structure of Your Business

For this subject matter of determining your business structure, I totally recommend that you consult an Accountant. It is important that you consider your tax saving options for your unique business. Below are the different types of legal structures one should consider when starting their business.

- Sole Proprietorship - A business owned and managed by one individual who is personally liable for all business debts and obligations.
- Partnership - A single business owned by two or more people.

- Corporation - A legal entity owned by shareholders.
- S-Corporation - A special type of corporation created through a tax election. An eligible domestic corporation can avoid double taxation (once to the shareholders and again to the corporation) by electing to be treated as an S corporation.
- Limited Liability Company (LLC) - A hybrid legal structure that provides the limited liability features of a corporation and the tax efficiencies and operational flexibility of a partnership.
- Non Profit - An organization engaged in activities of public or private interest where making a profit is not a primary mission. Some non-profits are exempt from paying federal taxes.
- 501(c) - A tax-exempt, nonprofit corporation

- Cooperative - A business or organization owned by and operated for the benefit of those using its services. Cooperatives are not a legal structure.

Registering Your Business

Register your business with your respective state and government agency in which you plan to do business. The information listed below is for Florida residents.

- Register your business with the required local, state, and federal government.
- Determine your corporation structure
- Choose your company business name
- Apply for any required business licenses
- State of Florida: www.sunbiz.org (Apply to your respective state agency) www.myflorida.com

- County: Determine occupational license and zoning, requirements, depending on your city and county requirement. Florida (www.orangecountyfl.net and/or www.cityoforlando.net)
- Taxes: Apply for an Employer Identification Number (www.irs.gov); Register with State of Florida (Or, your respective state.) sales tax-Florida Department of Revenue

Chapter Four Assignment

- ✞ Exercise at least 30 minutes per day for three days per week.
- ✞ Spend quality time with God each day thanking Him for His direction with your new business.
- ✞ Thank God for closing all doors that need to be closed and for opening doors that need to be opened in your life.
- ✞ Ask God for His grace through the transition and ask Him to provide a prayer partner and a mentor according to His will.
- ✞ Continue to embrace your new positive associations.
- ✞ Continue to formulate your Business Plan.
- ✞ Discuss and brainstorm your business name with your family members and mentor(s).
- ✞ Thank God for developing your hearing so you can hear His voice clearly.

🕊 Continue sowing seeds with your talents and offerings.

💰 Give your tithe (10% of all income you receive).

📖 Read Psalm 1 and Psalm 91 daily.

Chapter Five

How to Choose Your Business Location

Location is a key element to the success of your business. When choosing your business location asking yourself the following questions can alleviate a lot of stress and future problems:

- What is the nature of your business?
- Can you conduct your business from your home legally?
- Do you need high foot traffic?
- What are the costs for local taxes, utility rates, and shopping center fees?
- Is my landlord flexible and cooperative?
- Can I make changes to the building to accommodate my products and services?
- Is it a safe environment for both my customers and my staff?

- Is there anything I need to know about the areas I plan to start my business? (Always speak with current business owners within the proximity of the area where you are considering starting your business.)
- Visit the location where you plan to start your business during different times of the day, particularly during the morning, noon, and late evening. This will give you a more accurate understanding of the environment.
- What is the zoning and signage requirement for that location? Does the zoning permit your type of business at that location?
- What is the proximity to your closest competitors?
- Shop your closest competitor and observe their service, business volume and their customers. Remember, we are Christian business owners; therefore, we should operate with integrity. We

are not there to steal customers, we are only there to observe.

- Will your customers have easy access to your business?
- What is the AM and PM traffic flow like? Are you located on the appropriate side of the street to attract traffic flow?
- Does the location fit the nature of your business and the image that your company is trying to create with its customers?

Chapter Five Assignment

- Exercise at least 35 minutes per day for five days per week.
- Spend quality time with God each day thanking Him for His direction with your new business.
- Thank God for closing all doors that need to be closed and for opening doors that need to be opened in your life.
- Thank God for His grace through this transition period.
- Continue to embrace your new positive associations.
- Continue to formulate your Business Plan. Start to research your local SCORE office and make contact with the Small Business Administration office, which will assist you with your Business Plan.

- Discuss and brainstorm your business name with your family members and mentor(s).
- Thank God for developing your hearing so you can hear His voice clearly. Spend quiet time with God daily.

🕊 Continue sowing seeds with your talents and offerings.

💰 Give your tithe (10% of all income you receive).

📖 Read Psalm 1 and Psalm 91 daily.

Chapter Six

Positioning Your Business for Success

Advertizing and Marketing Your Business

By now, you should have decided on your company name. Research the name you have chosen for your respective state business website: For example, the website for The Department of State Division of Corporations in Florida is at www.sunbiz.org. For your respective state, do an Internet search for the "Department of State" and enter the state where you will operate your business. If you are still having difficulty creating your company name and/or website address, go to a library and have a librarian show you how to research company names and website addresses online.

Once you have determined that the name you have chosen is still available, proceed with registering your company name. I recommend that you have an accountant register your company name for you, especially if this is the first business your have registered. If not, carefully complete the necessary documentations discussed in "Registering Your Business" section. Once you have registered your company name, received confirmation that your new business name is now registered, and received your EIN (Federal Employee Identification Number, http://www.irs.gov), go to your local city and county tax office. They will inform you about what taxes you need to pay, the frequency you need to pay taxes and if any additional professional licenses are required to operate your business. You will need the EIN to get a checking account at most banks.

Congratulations! You are on your way to becoming a new business owner. Once you have completed the required documentation per law, it is time to proceed with marketing your business.

1. Create business cards and flyers with easy to read fonts. Your business cards and flyers should include:
    i. Your Company Name
    ii. Your Name
    iii. Your Business Address
    iv. Your Business Telephone Number
    v. Your Business Fax Number
    vi. Your Business E-mail Address
    vii. Your Business Website
2. Tell everyone that will listen to you about your business. They might not be able to use your services but they can refer you to someone that will.

3. Place an advertisement in your local newspaper's business section. This is sometimes free.
4. Send flyers out to businesses/residents within a thirty-mile radius of your business. Speak with your local post office representatives and they will assist you.
5. Find large shopping centers within a five-mile radius of your business and place flyers on vehicles, or distribute flyers to people leaving the major department stores. You should be able to pay a reliable high school student to do this. Make sure you are not breaking your respective city laws with your guerilla marketing efforts.
6. Speak with local school administrators and your church representatives about placing an ad in their bulletin.

7. Attend at least two networking events per week and start to promote your business.
8. Sponsor a charitable event. Make sure the ROI (Return on Investment) is worth it. Measure the number of attendees and make sure they are among your targeted customers.
9. Join professional organizations that support your specific type of business.
10. Internet search and research all free local advertising agencies.
11. Ask your bank official if you may set up a table in their lobby to promote your new business at least twice a month for three months. Your banker would definitely love to see your business flourish so get their input on how they can help you advertise.

Social Media

1. Pay a professional to create a website that represents your company image. Research other websites within your line of business. This will give you a better idea of how you want yours to look.
2. Create a Facebook® account. If you are not sure how, give this project to your young teenage or young adult children, nieces, nephews, or cousins.
3. Creating a Twitter® account is another fabulous idea. Make sure you will have the time to blog and keep up with the communications required. Remember, this is a reflection on your business so you need to maintain the image you are trying to portray.
4. Attend a social media workshop, especially one that is presented by your local SBA (Small Business Administration), SCORE, or chamber office.

Chapter Six Assignment

- ✟ Exercise at least 40 minutes per day for five days per week.
- ✟ Spend quality time with God each day thanking Him for His direction with your new business.
- ✟ Thank God for closing all doors that need to be closed and for opening doors that need to be opened in your life.
- ✟ Thank God for His grace through this transition period.
- ✟ Thank God for your new positive associations.
- ✟ Thank God for giving you the desire to have a prayer partner and mentor in your life.
- ✟ Thank God for developing your hearing so you can hear His voice clearly and spend quiet time with Him daily.

🕊 Continue sowing seeds with your talents and offerings. Remember, you cannot out-give God).

💰 Give your tithe (10% of all income you receive).

📖 Read Psalm 1 and Psalm 91 daily.

Chapter Seven

Selecting a Successful Team

Congratulations, your business is flourishing and now you need to hire some good help. Listed below are some guidelines to follow so you can reduce staffing costs and at the same time maintain a productive staff.

Making the Right Hiring Decisions

Here are some pointers to consider when hiring your staff.

- Determine the type of help you need.
- Determine the required experience this person should have.
- How many hours will he or she have to work per day and per week?
- Do you have or project to have funds available to cover payroll expenses for your employees?
- Once you have determined that you truly need additional help then move forward by advertising your need for help.

Now you are ready to proceed with interviews

- Schedule quality time (at least one hour of uninterrupted time) to interview candidates.
- Have all applicants complete an employment application. Create an application for your own use. There are free Employment

Applications online. You can check with your local Department of Labor or Workforce Office to see if your application meets state and federal standards.

- Employment applications should include an "At will" clause that states either party can terminate the employment agreement at will and with no liability.
- Have at least one other person you trust interview the candidate independently. If it is a management position, have at least three interviewers.
- Record answers to your questions during your interviews.
- Have no distractions during interviews (i.e., phone calls.)
- Ask open-ended questions. (Questions that require more than a yes or no answer)

- Listen for previous employment behaviors and consider them future behaviors.
- Pay attention to body language. The candidate should be able to look you in the eye when responding to your questions. If he or she fails to do so chances are the candidate is not telling the truth, or is possibly hiding something. Some cultures do not make direct eye contact with superiors, consider this before rejecting the candidate.
- Listen for team player clues.
- Evaluate the most qualified person versus the most suitable person for a position. Are you willing to hire someone that has all the required credentials and no work history, versus someone who has the proven work history and no credentials?

- Adhere to established hiring practices and be consistent with all applicants. Do not show favoritism.
- Always check references and check a minimum of three references.
- Consistency with employees minimizes discrimination lawsuits. If you conduct background checks and require drug testing, do the same for all employees. Check with your state for up to date labor laws.
- Have an established wage scale and be consistent with all employees.

Maintaining Your Workforce

- Orientate your new-hires on job responsibilities. This should take place prior to putting your new team members to work. During orientation you should also talk with

your new team members regarding your business:
- o History
- o Vision
- o Mission
- o Company Policies
  - Dress Code
  - Probationary Period
  - Pay Period (Weekly or Bi-weekly) verify your state law requirements.
  - Progressive Discipline
  - Holiday pay
  - Tardiness
  - Misconduct
  - Solicitation
  - Harassment
  - Vacation pay
  - Associate incentives
  - Who are your customers?

- What is great customer service for your business?
- How do you keep your customers coming back and how does it correlate to his or her wages. The more profit the more job security.
  - Have an established employee recognition program in place. You can start by awarding your team members who have gone over and beyond the call of duty with a small token of appreciation. This is not to be mistaken with an employee who just simply does their job.
  - Celebrate success and communicate failure.
  - Solicit your employees' ideas and keep a system in place to show that you have implemented or plan to implement their ideas, or explain why it might not be the

appropriate time to implement the idea. Be positive when communicating this so that your team members will not lose interest in participating in this program.
- Compliment employees in public and discipline them behind closed doors.
- Invest in your employees by giving them health benefits and education reimbursement whenever you can afford to do so. The ROI (Return on Investment) will be worth it.
- Get to know your employees professionally.
- Be a positive role model to your employees and respect them. When they speak with you confidentially let it remain that way. Do not tell their business to other team members.

Employer's Legal Responsibilities

- Maintain accurate I-9 records for employees. Always check with your local Workforce Office for any changes with the I-9 documentation process. You will need to complete and turn in accurate documentation within three days from the date of hire.
- Maintain a safe work environment for yourself and your employees.
- Communicate with your employees regarding their pay period (daily/weekly/bi-weekly/monthly).
- Complete federal income tax withholdings documentation annually. Consult your local government for any additional documentation that needs to be completed by you and your employees.

- Treat all employees fairly. Be consistent with your policies and procedures.
- Know your state laws regarding workers compensation, labor laws, and payroll.
- Allow your team members to mentor newer members of your team.

Chapter Seven Assignment

- Exercise at least 45 minutes per day for four days per week.
- Spend quality time with God each day thanking Him for His direction with your new business.
- Thank God for closing all doors that need to be closed and for opening doors that need to be opened in your life.
- Thank God for His grace through this transition period.
- Thank God for your new positive associations.
- Thank God for giving you the desire to have a prayer partner and mentor in your life.
- Continue to formulate your Business Plan.

- Research local Chambers of Commerce and schedule your first networking event. At this point, you are attending only to observe.
- Research the company name you have chosen on your local business administration website. Recommendation: Seek an accountant's assistance when registering your business name.
- Thank God for developing your hearing so you can hear His voice clearly.

🕊 Continue sowing seeds with your talents and offerings.

💰 Give your tithe (10% of all earnings you receive).

📖 Read Psalm 1 and Psalm 91 daily.

Chapter Eight

Your Business Startup Expense (Accounting)

Complete the following information below which will give you a true picture of what you need to start your business. Some areas may not apply to your respective business.

Startup Expenses

Basis of Capital

Owners' Investment:

<u>Names</u>	<u>Percent of Ownership</u>
You	
Partner	
Partner	

Bank Loans

    Other Loan Sources

    Startup Expenses

Real Estate/Building

    Construction

    Purchases

    Remodeling

    Other

Leasehold Improvements

Capital Equipment

    Furniture

    Equipment

    Fixtures

    Machinery

Location and Administrative Expenses

    Rental Equipment

    Utility Deposits

    Legal and Accounting Fees

    Prepaid Insurance

    Pre-Opening Salaries

Opening Inventory

Advertising and Marketing Expenses

    Advertising

    Signage

    Printing

    Additional Signage

Other Expenses

Chapter Eight Assignment

- Exercise at least 45 minutes per day for four days per week.
- Spend quality time with God each day thanking Him for His direction with your new business.
- Thank God for His grace through this transition period.
- Select a mentor and a prayer partner. Do not be in a rush to do so if your spirit doesn't lead you
- Attend a Networking Event (at this point you should already be promoting your business).
- Continue to formulate your Business Plan.
- Congrats, you have now selected a company name for your business.

- Research for local companies that offer free business promotion.
- Thank God for developing your hearing so you can hear His voice clearly. Spend quiet time with God daily.

🕊 Continue sowing seeds with your talents and offerings.

💰 Give your tithe (10% of all earnings you receive).

📖 Psalm 1 and Psalm 91 daily.

Chapter Nine

Growing Your Business

Successful Networking

In order to build a successful business you need a great customer/client base. Since your business is new and you are trying to build your customer base, I would recommend that you attend at least one Networking Event per week. Be more concerned about building a business relationship rather than just handing out business cards.

Remember, a recommendation is always better than a referral. It is also a good idea to volunteer your time with charitable organizations because in order to reap a harvest you have to sow seeds first.

Getting Prepared for a Networking Event

- ✟ Proper hygiene is important. You want your space to be welcoming. Do not wear overpowering cologne or perfume.
- ✟ Wear a dark colored suit (Black, brown or dark blue). Note: you do not want your clothes to be a distraction; instead, you want people to pay attention to what you have to say.
- ✟ Invest in a Name Badge. It looks more professional. Your name badge should have your name, and your company name. Your name badge should be worn on the top right of your jacket for easy visibility.

- ✝ Make-up should be worn in moderation; again, do not wear anything that will be a distraction.
- ✝ Women--no purses. Wear a suit with pockets to keep your business cards on hand. Keep all business cards you receive as your beginning network base. Develop a system of putting all business cards you receive from others in your left pocket and keep your business cards in your right pocket. This way you will not accidently give away someone's business card while thinking it was your own.
- ✝ Remember to use a firm handshake and maintain good eye contact because this will validate that you are a strong and serious business owner.
- ✝ Take notes on business cards you receive.

- "Divide and conquer!" When attending a networking event with your business partner (spouse, child, friend), you should work the room independently. This will give you the opportunity to meet more potential clients/customers.
- Spend five minutes maximum with each prospect. Remember, this is not a social gathering; it is all about business.
- Know your elevator speech. This is a precise, well-rehearsed description of your product and/or service. The elevator speech concept proposes that anyone should be able to understand your business in the time it would take to ride an elevator one floor.
- Reminder: The best way to sell is not to sell. It is best to build a business relationship first because a recommendation is better than a referral.

Chapter Nine Assignment

✝ Exercise at least one hour per day for four days per week.
✝ Spend quality time with God each day thanking Him for His divine favor and divine connections for your new business.
✝ Thank God for His grace through this transition period.
✝ Select a mentor and a prayer partner. If you are not comfortable with anyone you know continue to praise God for one anyway. Do not rush this process.
✝ Attend at least two networking events per month. Always pray for divine connections and favor from God before you attend these events.
✝ Continue to formulate your Business Plan. Have a professional a representative from your local Score or SBA (Small Business

Administration) office to review your Business Plan.

✟ Think about members in your family, church, and community that you might be able to employ in your business. Pray to God for guidance through this process.

✟ Find local companies that offer free businesses promotion, make sure they are reputable companies.

✟ Thank God for speaking to you and submit yourself to His will.

🕊 Continue sowing seeds with your talents and offerings.

💰 Give your tithe (10% of all income you receive).

📖 Read Psalm 1 and Psalm 91 daily.

Chapter Ten

Stay Encouraged

Now that you have started your business(es) here are some reminders of which you should never lose focus.

You must have a personal relationship with God through:

- ✟ Prayer
- ✟ Fasting
- ✟ Meditation of God's Word
- ✟ Spending quiet, uninterrupted time alone
- ✟ Spending quiet, uninterrupted time with God
- ✟ Each day ask God for your assignment that day and ask Him to help you not to miss your visitations and divine appointments.

- ✞ Worship and Praise God
- ✞ Celebrate your milestone achievements.
- ✞ You must continue to sow seeds
- ✞ Your time
- ✞ Your finances
- ✞ Your talents

Introduce this ministry (How to Turn Your Talent into a Business) to at least two people who need to start their own business.

As you climb the ladder of success become a mentor to someone else (pass the torch).

You must stay faithful!

As you wait for your breakthrough, volunteer your time at charitable organizations near your area.

Form a Prayer Warrior Team (PWT) for yourself. This is a list of at least two people you can call anytime to pray, fast, and intercede for you. These people should function more as your spiritual confidants. You should be able to share your unedited feelings with them.

Build Your Networking Group

Reminder Christians are not the only people that do businesses, however, never compromise your faith for a dollar. Expand your business circle.

- Get involved with local Chambers and charitable organizations.
- Allow yourself to be in the presence of positive people and successful business owners.
- Attend at least two networking events per week.
- Stay connected with me, your mentor, your prayer partner, and prayer warriors.

- Create a monthly support group for Kingdom Business Owners.

As you have now gone through valleys, experienced what it means to trust in God. I am sure at this point you have several testimonies. Yes, you went through a test so you could have a testimony. Now you can be a witness to how great God is. This is your season to sore, to see the manifestation of your harvest. Stay focused and always remembers that God's grace is on your life. Be sure to share your testimony with others so that others can be helped. Remember, God blesses us to be a blessing to others, so remember to share the wealth.

As you continue to maintain an excellent relationship with your loyal customers do not become complacent about their loyalty. Always seek new ways to motivate them. Have incentive programs in place for them, just as you would your new customers.

I believe the process of starting your business is much like being a pregnant woman. During the first trimester, the pregnant woman goes through the phase of what we call "Morning sickness." She is nauseous, yet excited. In the same way, aspiring business owners during their first couple of months in business become very anxious and nervous all at once. They sometimes ask themselves, "Am I doing the right thing?"

Both the pregnant woman and the aspiring business owners continue to plan for that big day that they will give birth. The business owner will give birth to a new business while the pregnant woman will give birth to a child. Both will go through the exciting stage one buying clothes for her new born the other selecting business name for his or her new business, and sharing the idea of opening a new business both are so excited and happy.

As the birthing stage draws near both the pregnant woman and the aspiring business owner start to feel tension. In both cases, the tension stems from something within them that needs to give birth or come forth. The pregnant woman can touch her stomach and feel the baby inside her. She talks to it and comforts it. The aspiring business owner has God to speak to confirming that he or she knows that God will help them to birth their new ideas. This is where faith can separate the two. The pregnant woman has not seen what is inside of her but she trusts her doctor that it is a baby. Therefore, she treats her pregnancy as if she is carrying a human being in her womb. How much more should we trust God that whatever He has impregnated us with we will also give birth to?

When a pregnant woman goes into labor, she pushes her way through the pain. The first stage might include contractions that are thirty minutes apart. Because she already prepared herself for this moment, she knows what breathing technique to use to relieve her pain. As the contractions get closer together, she knows to push harder and longer. At no point does she ever quit. She knows something is inside of her that needs to be birthed. As she pushes through the pain with her mother on her left side and her husband on her right side, she knows she still has to do the work. The tougher the pain the harder she knows she has to push.

On the other hand, an aspiring business owner starts to feel challenged. This might be due to the stress of getting all the required permits passed for the new building, or not being able to get approval for the loan they need to buy the necessary equipment for the store. It might be that the owner has not been able to find the perfect location for the business, and it is at this stage that the aspiring business owner may become weary and start to question him/herself by thinking, "Am I doing the right thing?" This is where most aspiring business owners fail or quit. They do not push themselves as the woman in labor would. They just throw in the towel or even let their dream fade away. Don't you know it is the plan of the devil to put up roadblocks just as you are about to cross the finish line of one level, which would then transcend you into another level? Just as a woman in labor pushes her way through the pain, so should you. The stronger the pain the harder you should Push! Push! Push! If you feel you cannot push anymore bring out all your weapons, its wartime and God is with you so you will conquer in Jesus name.

1. Our Bible has a verse for all situations. Speak God's words over your situation. "No weapon formed against [me] shall prosper (Isaiah 54:17 KJV)" "Through God all things are possible." "I am the lender and not the barrower." "I live by faith, and not by sight," "By Your favor, Lord, You have established me a strong mountain." Speak God's Word until they come alive.
2. Call your prayer warrior and unite with her/im through prayer and fasting.
3. Never give up on God's will for your life.

Your challenges build your experience pool that turns you into an expert in your field. So embrace your setbacks and consider them your downtime for better preparation. Use them as your steps to another level of greatness. When you have done everything, you are supposed to do be still and trust God. His timing is not our timing. He is always on time. God is never late. Always believe His words. He never lies. His words are final. You will be successful if you trust God.

Thanks to the Following

Dr. Zachery Tims
New Destiny Christian Center
505 East McCormick Ave
Apopka, Florida 32707
407-884-6322
www.ndcc.tv

New Destiny Christian Center
Entrepreneur Ministry
destinybusiness@ndcc.tv

Ms Sonia Troupe
Fromtheheart Photography
troupetrouper@aol.com
407-470-9072

Author
Janet Green
PO Box 691966
Orlando Fl 32869
407-925-1652
www.janetbusiness.com
howto@janetbusiness.com

When Emailing: Please include a testimony of any insights you have received from this book.

Dear Reader,

I would like personally to thank our Pastor Dr. Zachery Tims, Jr. for being the visionary that he is in allowing the Entrepreneur Ministry to be a blessing to current and future business owners within our congregation and the community.

I would like to express my sincere appreciation to Janet Green for doing a remarkable job with the Entrepreneur Ministry at New Destiny Christian Center. Through her tireless efforts she has created an environment where visionaries can walk out their long life dreams of becoming business owners. Ms. Green seeks out training and informational opportunities within the community and incorporates those resources right into the entrepreneur ministry with the scope of helping student's who attend the training program benefit from the networking events, business showcasing events and the gala events that are put on by the ministry.

The classes that Ms. Green puts on are created to provide both established and start up businesses the resources necessary to grow their business. Whether through learning how to complete applications to solicit government grant monies or contracts through the city development commission or how to file to obtain a tax ID number Ms. Green is hard at work trying to connect entrepreneurs with established businesses and existing chambers in hopes of getting entrepreneur's on the way to success.

Our business Millennium Solutions has profited a great deal from the networking events and the training that we've been exposed to through the Entrepreneur Ministry at New Destiny Christian Center. I highly recommend that everyone whether a current business owner or not should attend the events and get ignited. Refuel your fire, when you come together with other people just as yourself who are working at getting to the next level in business I promise it will be a changing experience.

Thank you,

Roosevelt and Luz Adams
of Millennium Solutions Corp.

Index

1 Corinthians 3
16 32
1 Corinthians 6
19 32
1 Peter 5
7 43
2 Corinthians 11
27 34
2 Corinthians 6
16 32
2 Corinthians 9
8 43
3 John 1
2 45
Deuteronomy 28
1 45
12 45
8 43
Deuteronomy 8
18 .... 22, 42
Ephesians 4
6-8 23
Galatians 5
22-26 29
Genesis 8
22 35
Isaiah 1
19 23
Isaiah 40
29 34
Isaiah 54
17 44
Isaiah 54:17 132
James 2
14 30
John 14
13-14 40
Leviticus 27
30 33
Luke 1
28 42
Luke 5
1-7 36
Luke 6
38 42
Malachi 3
10-11 44
8 33
Matthew 17
20 41
21 34
Matthew 5
23-24 33
44 30
Matthew 6
14 30
Matthew 7
7-8 41

Proverbs 10
22 43
Proverbs 11
27 41
Proverbs 3
9 33
Psalm 1
3 43
Psalm 112
3 42
Psalm 37
4 .... 22, 44
5 35
Read Psalm 23 50
Romans 12
14-19 31

Notes:

_____
_____
_____
_____
_____
_____
_____
_____
_____
_____
_____
_____
_____
_____
_____
_____
_____

www.ingramcontent.com/pod-product-compliance
Lightning Source LLC
LaVergne TN
LVHW051839080426
835512LV00018B/2972